WHAT KINDS OF SEEDS ARE THESE?

The illustrations were created using watercolor and gouache on Arches watercolor paper
The text and display type were set in Shannon and Nyx
Composed in the United States of America
Designed by Lois A. Rainwater
Edited by Kristen McCurry
Author photo © The Picture People

NORTHWORD

Books for Young Readers
11571 K-Tel Drive
Minnetonka, MN 55343
www.tnkidsbooks.com

Library of Congress Cataloging-in-Publication Data

Roemer, Heidi.
What kinds of seeds are these? / by Heidi Bee Roemer ; illustrated by Olena Kassian.

p. cm.

ISBN 1-55971-955-9 (hardcover)
1. Seeds--Dispersal--Juvenile literature. 2. Seeds--Juvenile literature. I. Kassian, Olena, ill. II. Title.

QK929.R64 2006

581.4'67--dc22

2005038049

Printed in Singapore
10 9 8 7 6 5 4 3 2 1

To Ric, who believes
in the promise of a seed
—H. B. R.

To my sister,
who shares my love for all things
green and growing
—O. K.

WHAT KINDS OF
SEEDS
ARE THESE?

by
HEIDI BEE ROEMER

illustrated by
OLENA KASSIAN

NORTHWORD
Minnetonka, Minnesota

Seeds are floaters and fliers and buried-alivers,
exploders and sticklers and hitchhiking tricksters.
Seeds travel around in their clever disguises.
There are billions of seeds—
and they're full of surprises!

When chubby worms wriggle and robins sing, "Spring!"
these trees produce seeds with propeller-shaped wings.
Whirling and twirling, they whif-whuffle down.
These angel-winged seeds will
soon sprout from the ground.

What kinds of seeds are these?

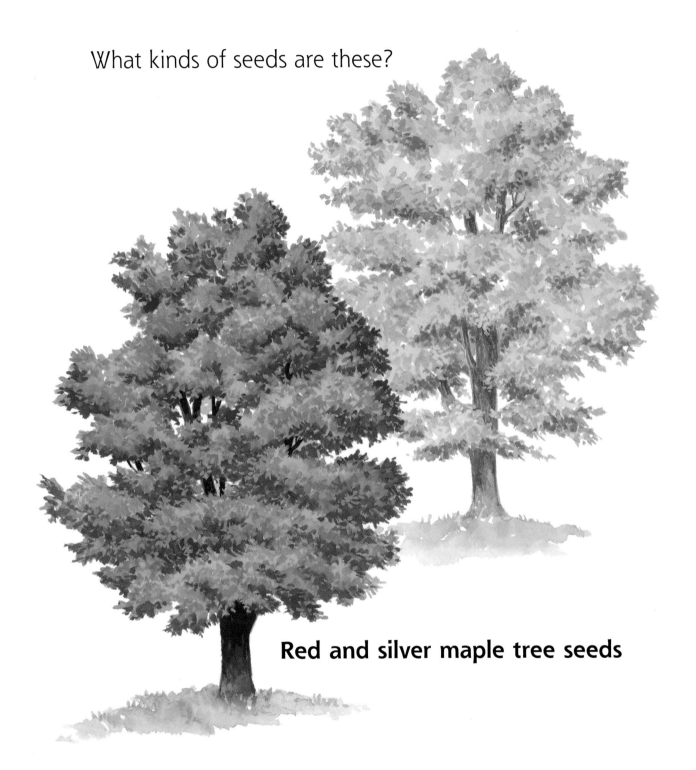

Red and silver maple tree seeds

They tumble from palm trees and roll to the ocean,
bob like a boat with an up-and-down motion,
drift out to sea 'til they're
washed up on shore,
then sprout—and begin their
lifecycle once more!

What kind of seed is this?

A coconut from a palm tree

Wedged like peas in a pod or sardines in a tin,
these seeds are contained in canoe-style skins.
When the skin gets too tight, little seeds get a squeeze—
they pop from their pod like a miniature sneeze!

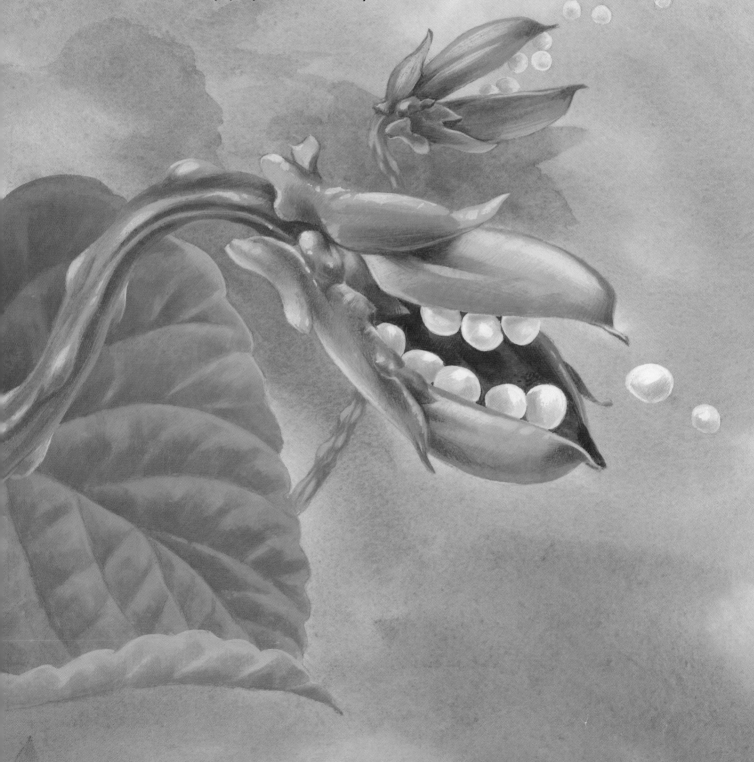

What kind of seed is this?

A violet seed

If you walk in the woods
where the brush grows up thick,
don't be surprised
if you snag seeds that prick.
Like fishhooks or Velcro,
they stick where they're stuck.
Have you tried to remove
these hitchhikers?
Good luck!

What kind of seed is this?

A burr from a great burdock

Wispy-soft tufts made of cottonlike fluff
are light as a feather; they wait for a puff.
Each parachute carries its own little seed—
away the tufts drift on a soft summer breeze.

What kind of seed is this?

A dandelion seed carried by a dandelion pappus

Birds, bats, and mice often gobble fruit up—but
fruit seeds may cruise through a critter's small gut.
Those not digested come out again, whole!
If they're dropped in soft soil, they may start to grow!

What kind of seed is this?

A blackberry seed

After their blossoms have withered and died,
these plants become brittle, the sun bakes them dry.
They roll on the ground, blown by winds that are strong,
scattering seeds as they tumble along.

What kind of seed is this?

A Russian thistle seed carried by a tumbleweed

Like small bits of dirt or specks of black pepper,
these oh-so-small seeds are unusual trekkers.
When moistened, these seeds become gummy as glue.
Some gel-coated seeds may be stuck to your shoe!

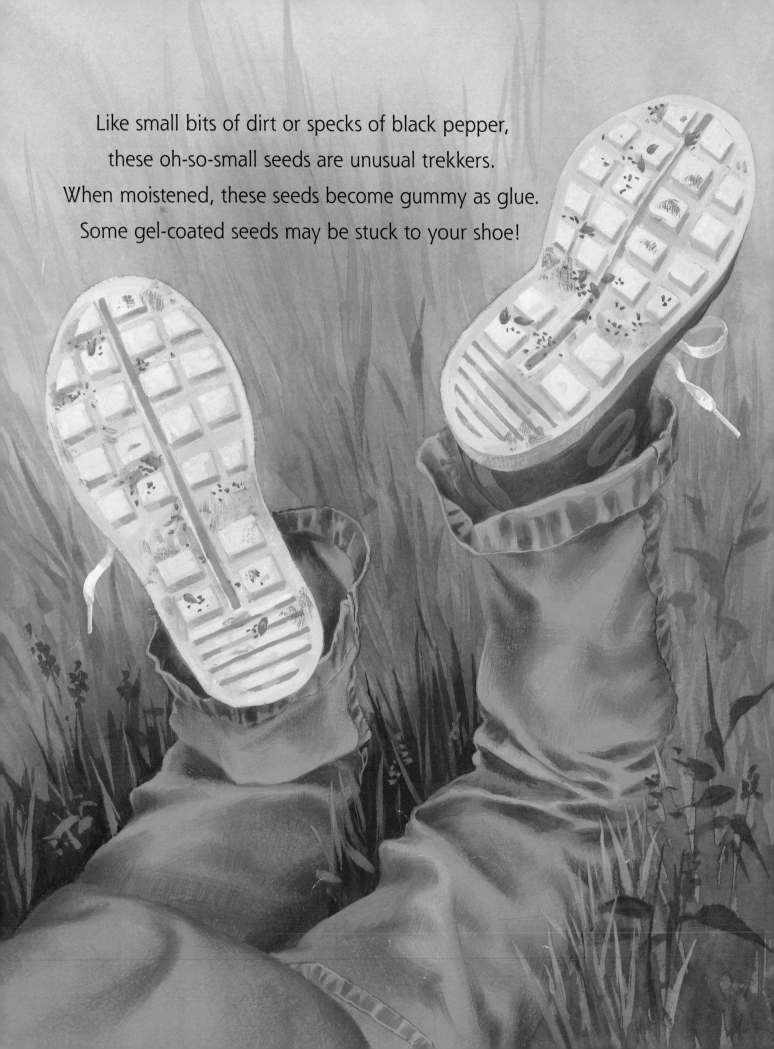

What kind of seed is this?

A broad-leaved plantain seed

Winter is coming; squirrel scampers and toils.
He busily buries these seeds in the soil.
And if squirrel forgets where he's hidden his seeds,
they may sprout and grow a whole forest of trees!

What kind of seed is this?

An acorn from an oak tree

Grow Your Own Fun with Seeds!

In spring or fall...

Make "Mystery Seed Socks!" To protect your feet, put on a pair of flip-flops or sandals, then pull an old pair of Mom or Dad's socks over the shoes. Go for a walk in a field, woods, or forest. Seeds, brambles, and burrs

will stick to your socks. At home, remove the socks and examine the seeds. How many different seeds do you find? You might even try planting the socks in a pot of dirt. Place it near sunlight and water lightly every day. See what mysterious plants begin to sprout!

Anytime...

Make "Seed Heads!" Draw faces of friends or family members on Styrofoam cups. (Or, perhaps a witch's face for Halloween or another fun holiday face.) Unroll cotton and stuff it into the cups, or use cotton balls. Pour enough water over the cotton to get it really wet. Sprinkle cress seeds on top of the cotton.

Place the cups near a window and keep seeds moist. In a few days, the seeds will sprout cress plant "hair." Give your gift-plants to friends—and keep one for yourself! Cress may be chopped and sprinkled on eggs for breakfast. Yum!

Invent a seed...

Invent your own "Seed-on-the-Go!" How will your seed get where it needs to be? Will it have flippers, paddles, or a parachute? Will it stick to passersby like chewing gum, or will it launch like a rocket? Will it fall from a tree or pass through an animal's body? What kind of plant will it sprout? Get out your art supplies and use your imagination!

HEIDI BEE ROEMER sprouted a green thumb at a young age. She and her dad grew pumpkins so humongous, she couldn't put her arms around them! Nowadays, when Heidi isn't fertilizing azaleas or plucking huckleberries, she teaches writers' workshops, works as an instructor for The Institute of Children's Literature, and serves as an advisor for the Society of Children's Book Writers and Illustrators. This is Heidi's second book. She and her husband live near Chicago and have two college-age sons.

OLENA KASSIAN has illustrated sixteen books and written three. She attended the Ontario College of Art at the University of Guelph in Canada and worked in advertising for many years before beginning her career in children's books. When she's not holding a paintbrush or exhibiting her work, Olena loves gardening, reading, bicycling, and traveling around the world. Olena has two grown children and lives with her partner in Toronto, Ontario.